Ninja Foodi Air Fryer Cookbook UK #2023

Delicious Air Fry, Dehydrate, Roast, Bake, Reheat, and More Recipes for Beginners and Advanced Users

Caitlin Bibi

Copyright ©2022 By Caitlin Bibi All rights reserved.

No part of this guide may be reproduced in any form without permission in writing from the publisher except in the case of brief quotations embodied in critical articles or reviews.

Legal & Disclaimer

The information contained in this book and its contents is not designed to replace or take the place of any form of medical or professional advice; and is not meant to replace the need for independent medical, financial, legal or other professional advice or services, as may be required. The content and information in this book has been provided for educational and entertainment purposes only.

The content and information contained in this book has been compiled from sources deemed reliable, and it is accurate to the best of the Author's knowledge, information and belief. However, the Author cannot guarantee its accuracy and validity and cannot be held liable for any errors and/or omissions. Further, changes are periodically made to this book as and when needed. Where appropriate and/or necessary, you must consult a professional (including but not limited to your doctor, attorney, financial advisor or such other professional advisor) before using any of the suggested remedies, techniques, or information in this book.

Contents

Introduction	06
Breakfast And Brunch Recipes	10
Egg & Potato Hash	11
Bell Pepper Omelet	12
Bacon & Spinach Muffins	13
Sweet Potato Tots	14
French Toast Sticks	15
Sausage Patties	16
Roasted Cauliflower	17
Tomato Quiche	18
Breakfast Frittata	19
Snack & Dessert Recipes	20
Vanilla Cheesecake	21
Cheddar Biscuits	22
Glazed Figs	23
Red Velvet Cupcakes	24
Air Fryer Lumpia	25
Gluten-free Cherry Crumble	26
Apple Fritters	27
Banana Split	28
Spicy Chickpeas	29
Poultry Recipes	30
Turkish Chicken Kebab	31
Spiced Chicken Thighs	32
Air Fryer Egg Rolls	33
Thyme Duck Breast	34
Herbed Turkey Breast	35
Marinated Chicken Thighs	36
Blackened Chicken Breast	37

Roasted Cornish Game Hen 38

Meat Recipes 39

Mushrooms With Steak 40

Pork Skewers With Mango Salsa & Black Bean 41

Braised Lamb Shanks 42

Buttered Rib Eye Steak 43

Beef Sirloin Roast 44

Air-fried Meatloaf 45

Pork Stuffed Bell Peppers 46

Glazed Pork Tenderloin 47

Fish & Seafood Recipes 48

Buttered Salmon 49

Seasoned Catfish 50

Lemony Shrimp 51

Spiced Tilapia 52

Zesty Fish Fillets 53

Cod Parcel 54

Ranch Tilapia 55

Pesto Salmon 56

Vegetarian And Vegan Recipes 57

Potato Gratin 58

Baked Potatoes 59

Potato-skin Wedges 60

Glazed Mushrooms 61

Sweet & Tangy Mushrooms 62

Roasted Vegetables 63

Spicy Butternut Squash 64

Fried Chickpeas 65

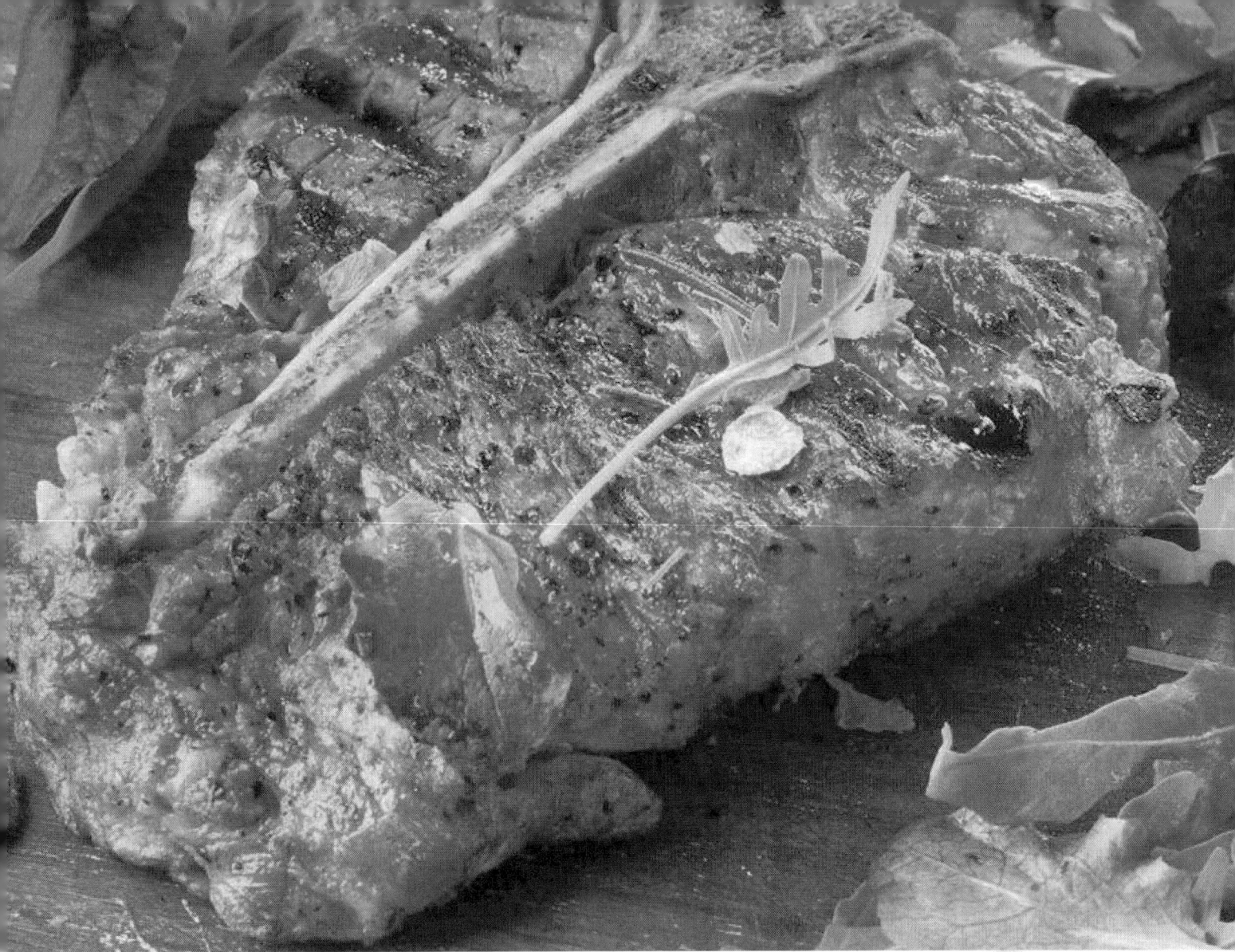

INTRODUCTION

The air fryer is a great tool on its own, but you can kick things up a notch when you use it with some other kitchen utensils you probably already have on hand. One of the dangers of air frying is overcooking the food you're making. With these tips, you'll avoid that problem and air fry like a pro! The air fryer obviously is a great way to prepare food in your kitchen, but have you ever thought about taking it on the road? With these tips, you'll be air frying wherever your wheels take you!

5 Kitchen Tools to Use with Your Air Fryer

Nothing is worse than buying a new appliance that requires you to spend an extra hundred bucks in special gadgets, right? Rest assured, the air fryer does not require you to do that! Using those kitchen tools you already have on hand, your air-fried foods will come to life. And even if you're not a cook and you need to invest in a few of the items listed here, they won't cost you an arm and a leg and you'll find multiple uses for them in your home.

Here are five air-fryer-friendly kitchen tools to have on hand:

- Silicone muffin liners: Make your muffins come to life with silicone muffin liners. Heat stable and perfectly portioned, silicone muffin liners allow you to bring the beauty of breads to the comfort of your own kitchen. Plus, you can even make baked eggs in them.
- Seven-inch springform (Bundt) pan: Cheesecakes and coffee cakes have a seat at your table when you invest in one of these (usually sold as a convertible cake and Bundt cake pan). You can enjoy a bakery-fresh slice of cake for less than a fraction of the cost.
- Seven-inch oven-safe casserole dish: Most air fryers don't exceed 400 degrees, meaning the same small casserole dish that withstands your oven temperatures will be safe in your air fryer, too. From glass to metal to silicone, the air fryer should accommodate them all!

Metal skewers: Take those skewers from the grill and use them in your air fryer to help evenly cook thicker cuts of meat. Depending on the type of air fryer you have, the skewers may (or may not) be too big for your fryer. If you're on the fence about skewers that will fit your air fryer, you can use wooden sticks (just be cautious of the temperature so you don't catch them on fire).

Kitchen tongs: Using a pair of kitchen tongs is essential to ensure you don't burn another finger trying to get that last chip that's nestled itself on the side of the fryer basket.

5 Ways to Prevent Air Frying Your Food to a Crisp

When cooking certain foods at high temperatures, charring can occur. That charring produces a chemical called acrylamide. And acrylamide might be linked to an increased risk of cancer. It's important to note that, according to the American Cancer Society, "It's not yet clear if the levels of acrylamide in foods raise cancer risk." Still, you can take some steps to avoid frying foods to a crisp. Here's what we recommend:

Cook at lower temperatures for longer periods of time (instead of high temperatures for shorter periods). Turning the temperature knob down to 300 to 325 degrees and increasing the time to 10 or 20 minutes may prevent charred coffee cake and blackened fries.

Cover foods with foil. The air fryer works to cook your foods by circulating air throughout the basket, so you don't want to prevent that air flow. However, you can use foil to cover a chicken breast, for example, and place it in the basket to cook (low and slow). We also suggest using foil to cover cakes and egg dishes to prevent the top from cooking too quickly. Just be sure there is enough room between the foil and the top of the air fryer.

Don't overfill the basket. You may be tempted to throw the entire batch of beet chips or broccoli florets into the basket at once to save time, but that will result in uneven cooking and a few pieces getting burned to a crisp. Either invest in a larger fryer or cook in smaller batches to produce the perfect air-fried foods every time.

Use air-fryer-safe equipment. The key to producing bakery-perfect muffins or quick breads lies in making sure you're using the right equipment. Using the right equipment helps allow the air to circulate properly, leaving your air-fried foods crisp, crunchy, and evenly cooked.

Set timers and reminders. We all need to set alarms to remember important things, and air frying your foods is no different. Set timers not only on your air fryer but on your phone so you don't leave the foods cooking any longer than required.

Air Frying on the Road

If you travel in an RV, you know space is tight. And yet many RVers are adding an air fryer to their tiny kitchens. Why? Because nothing beats an air fryer for reheating food with ease, making your favorite chicken wings without heating up your RV, and enjoying fresh baked cookies after a long day of hiking. But before you pack up, you need to understand the electrical requirements of both your vehicle and your air fryer, so be sure to review your camper's electrical needs first.

When you've determined that your air fryer will work in your vehicle, you're ready to get cooking! The following simple meals will be perfect for your next road trip:

- Chicken wings: This popular appetizer can be made in the comfort of your RV or camper in 22 minutes! Just season with salt and pepper and cook at 370 degrees for 22 minutes, flipping a couple times. Then finish off with your favorite hot sauce heated up with melted butter. Serve the wings with blue-cheese-stuffed celery, and call it a meal!

- Steak and potatoes: Who doesn't appreciate a good steak while taking in another stellar sunset? Dice potatoes and season with salt and pepper. Then cook at 360 degrees for 5 minutes. Season the steak with salt and pepper and place it in the air fryer basket next to the potatoes. Spray the food with cooking spray, crank up the heat to 390 degrees, and cook for 12 minutes, flipping the steak and shaking the potatoes after 6 minutes. Let the steak rest for 5 minutes, and serve with a simple salad to complete the meal.

- Crispy chimichangas: Whether it's for breakfast, lunch, or dinner, a chimichanga is an easy addition to your meal rotation. Try a simple bean and cheese chimichanga by spreading refried beans onto a tortilla, topping with shredded cheese, and rolling up like a sealed burrito. Spray the chimichanga with cooking spray and cook at 360 degrees for 8 to 10 minutes.

- BLT: Bacon comes out perfectly in an air fryer, without splattering grease all over your living space. Cook the bacon at 390 degrees for 8 to 10 minutes (or how you like it). Remove the bacon onto a paper towel. Then brush your bread with mayo and place it in the basket. Cook at 370 degrees for 2 minutes. Top with lettuce, tomato, and crispy bacon for a warm lunch!

- Frozen pizzas: Oh yes, that's right! You can now pick up your favorite frozen fare — from pizzas to Hot Pockets — at a grocery store instead of waiting in line at a restaurant. Be sure to pick up the individual sizes. Whip up a salad from a bag to complete the meal.

BREAKFAST AND BRUNCH RECIPES

Egg & Potato Hash

Servings: 1 / Cooking Time: 20 Mins.

Ingredients:

- 2 bacon slices, halved
- 2 small potatoes, chopped
- ¼ of tomato, chopped
- 1 egg
- 2 tbsp. cheddar cheese, shredded

Directions:

1. Arrange the bacon strips onto a double layer of tin foil.
2. Place the potatoes and tomato n top of the bacon.
3. Carefully crack the egg on top of the veggie mixture.
4. With the tin foil, shape the mixture into a bowl.
5. Press "Power Button" of Ninja Foodi Digital Air Fry Oven and turn the dial to select "Air Roast" mode.
6. Press "Time Button" and again turn the dial to set the cooking time to 20 minutes.
7. Now push "Temp Button" and rotate the dial to set the temperature at 350 degrees F.
8. Press "Start/Pause" button to start.
9. When the unit beeps to show that it is preheated, open the lid.
10. Carefully arrange the foil piece over the wire rack and insert in the oven.
11. After 16 minutes of cooking, top the hash with cheese.
12. When cooking time is complete, open the lid and transfer the foil pieces onto serving plates.
13. Serve hot.
14. Serving Suggestions: Garnishing of fresh parsley will enhance the taste of this potato hash.
15. Variation Tip: Use the right kind of potatoes.

Nutrition: **Calories: 326 Fat: 13.4g Sat Fat: 5.9g Carbohydrates: 36.8g Fiber: 5.6g Sugar: 3.4g Protein: 15.9g**

Bell Pepper Omelet

Servings: 2 / Cooking Time: 10 Mins.

Ingredients:

- 1 tsp. butter
- 1 small onion, sliced
- ½ of green bell pepper, seeded and chopped
- 4 eggs
- ¼ tsp. milk
- Salt and ground black pepper, as required
- ¼ C. Cheddar cheese, grated

Directions:

1. In a skillet, melt the butter over medium heat and cook the onion and bell pepper for about 4-5 minutes.
2. Remove the skillet from heat and set aside to cool slightly.
3. Meanwhile, in a bowl, add the eggs, milk, salt and black pepper and beat well.
4. Add the cooked onion mixture and gently, stir to combine.
5. Place the zucchini mixture into a small baking pan.
6. Press "Power Button" of Ninja Foodi Digital Air Fry Oven and turn the dial to select the "Air Fry" mode.
7. Press the Time button and again turn the dial to set the cooking time to 5 minutes.
8. Now push the Temp button and rotate the dial to set the temperature at 355 degrees F.
9. Press "Start/Pause" button to start.
10. When the unit beeps to show that it is preheated, open the lid.
11. Arrange pan over the "Wire Rack" and insert in the oven.
12. Cut the omelet into 2 portions and serve hot.

Nutrition: *Calories 223 Total Fat 15.5 g Saturated Fat 6.9 g Cholesterol 347 mg Sodium 304 mg Total Carbs 6.4 g Fiber 1.2 g Sugar 3.8 g Protein 15.3 g*

Bacon & Spinach Muffins

Servings: 17 / Cooking Time: 17 Mins.

Ingredients:

- 6 eggs
- ½ C. milk
- Salt and freshly ground black pepper, to taste
- 1 C. fresh spinach, chopped
- 4 cooked bacon slices, crumbled

Directions:

1. In a bowl, add the eggs, milk, salt and black pepper and beat until well combined.
2. Add the spinach and stir to combine.
3. Divide the spinach mixture into 6 greased C. of an egg bite mold evenly.
4. Press "Power Button" of Ninja Foodi Digital Air Fry Oven and turn the dial to select "Air Fry" mode.
5. Press "Time Button" and again turn the dial to set the cooking time to 17 minutes.
6. Now push "Temp Button" and rotate the dial to set the temperature at 325 degrees F.
7. Press "Start/Pause" button to start.
8. When the unit beeps to show that it is preheated, open the lid.
9. Arrange the mold over the wire rack and insert in the oven.
10. When cooking time is complete, open the lid and place the mold onto a wire rack to cool for about 5 minutes.
11. Top with bacon pieces and serve warm.
12. Serving Suggestions: Serve these muffins with the drizzling of melted butter.
13. Variation Tip: Don't forget to grease the egg bite molds before pacing the egg mixture in them.

Nutrition: *Calories: 179 Fat: 12.9g Sat Fat: 4.3g Carbohydrates: 1.8g Fiber: 0.1g Sugar: 1.3g Protein: 13.5g*

Sweet Potato Tots

Servings: 4 / Cooking Time: 1 Hour

Ingredients:

- 1 tbsp. of potato starch
- 2 small sweet potatoes, peeled
- 1-1/4 tsp. kosher salt
- 1/8 tsp. of garlic powder
- ¾ C. ketchup

Directions:

1. Boil water in a medium-sized pot over high heat.
2. Add the potatoes. Cook till it becomes tender. Transfer them to a plate for cooling. Grate them in a mid-sized bowl.
3. Toss gently with garlic powder, 1 tsp. of salt, and potato starch.
4. Shape the mix into tot-shaped cylinders.
5. Apply cooking spray on the air fryer basket.
6. Place half of the tots in a later in your basket. Apply some cooking spray.
7. Cook till it becomes light brown at 400°F.
8. Take out from the frying basket. Sprinkle some salt.
9. Serve with ketchup immediately.

Nutrition: Calories 80, Carbohydrates 19g, Total Fat 0g, Protein 1g, Fiber 2g, Sodium 335mg, Sugars 8g

French Toast Sticks

Servings: 2 / Cooking Time: 10 Mins.

Ingredients:

- 4 slices of thick bread
- 2 eggs, lightly beaten
- 1 tsp. cinnamon
- 1 tsp. of vanilla extract
- ¼ C. milk

Directions:

1. Cut the bread into slices for making sticks.
2. Keep parchment paper on the air fryer basket's bottom.
3. Preheat your air fryer to 180 degrees C or 360 degrees F.
4. Now stir together the milk, eggs, cinnamon, vanilla extract, and nutmeg (optional). Combine well.
5. Dip each bread piece into the egg mix. Submerge well.
6. Remove the excess fluid by shaking it well.
7. Keep them in the fryer basket in a single layer.
8. Cook without overcrowding your fryer.

Nutrition: Calories 241, Carbohydrates 29g, Cholesterol 188mg, Total Fat 9g, Protein 11g, Fiber 2g, Sodium 423mg, Sugars 4g

Sausage Patties

Servings: 4 / Cooking Time: 10 Mins.

Ingredients:

- 1 pack sausage patties
- 1 serving cooking spray

Directions:

1. Preheat your air fryer to 200 degrees C or 400 degrees F.
2. Keep the sausage patties in a basket. Work in batches if needed.
3. Cook for 3 minutes.
4. Turn the sausage over and cook for another 2 minutes.

Nutrition: Calories 168, Carbohydrates 1g, Cholesterol 46mg, Total Fat 12g, Protein 14g, Fiber 0g, Sodium 393mg, Sugars 1g

Roasted Cauliflower

Servings: 2 / Cooking Time: 15 Mins.

Ingredients:

- 4 C. of cauliflower florets
- 1 tbsp. peanut oil
- 3 cloves garlic
- ½ tsp. smoked paprika
- ½ tsp. of salt

Directions:

1. Preheat your air fryer to 200 degrees C or 400 degrees F.
2. Now cut the garlic into half. Use a knife to smash it.
3. Keep in a bowl with salt, paprika, and oil.
4. Add the cauliflower. Coat well.
5. Transfer the coated cauliflower to your air fryer.
6. Cook for 10 minutes. Shake after 5 minutes.

Nutrition: *Calories 136, Carbohydrates 12g, Cholesterol 0mg, Total Fat 8g, Protein 4g, Fiber 5.3g, Sodium 642mg, Sugars 5g*

Tomato Quiche

Servings: 2 / Cooking Time: 30 Mins.

Ingredients:

- 4 eggs
- ¼ C. onion, chopped
- ½ C. tomatoes, chopped
- ½ C. milk
- 1 C. Gouda cheese, shredded
- Salt, to taste

Directions:

1. In a small baking pan, add all the ingredients and mix well.
2. Press "Power Button" of Ninja Foodi Digital Air Fry Oven and turn the dial to select "Air Fry" mode.
3. Press "Time Button" and again turn the dial to set the cooking time to 30 minutes.
4. Now push "Temp Button" and rotate the dial to set the temperature at 340 degrees F.
5. Press "Start/Pause" button to start.
6. When the unit beeps to show that it is preheated, open the lid.
7. Arrange the pan over the wire rack and insert in the oven.
8. When cooking time is complete, open the lid and place the pan aside for about 5 minutes.
9. Cut into equal-sized wedges and serve.
10. Serving Suggestions: Fresh baby spring mix will be a great companion for this quiche.
11. Variation Tip: You can use any kind of fresh veggies for the filling of quiche.

Nutrition: *Calories: 247 Fat: 16.1g Sat Fat: 7.5g Carbohydrates: 7.3g Fiber: 0.9g Sugar: 5.2g Protein: 18.6g*

Breakfast Frittata

Servings: 2 / Cooking Time: 20 Mins.

Ingredients:

- 4 eggs, beaten lightly
- 4 oz. sausages, cooked and crumbled
- 1 onion, chopped
- 2 tbsp. of red bell pepper, diced
- ½ C. shredded Cheddar cheese

Directions:

1. Bring together the cheese, eggs, sausage, onion, and bell pepper in a bowl.
2. Mix well.
3. Preheat your air fryer to 180 degrees C or 360 degrees F.
4. Apply cooking spray lightly.
5. Keep your egg mix in a prepared cake pan.
6. Now cook in your air fryer till the frittata has become set.

Nutrition: *Calories 487, Carbohydrates 3g, Cholesterol 443mg, Total Fat 39g, Protein 31g, Fiber 0.4g, Sodium 694mg, Sugars 1g*

SNACK & DESSERT RECIPES

Vanilla Cheesecake

Servings: 6 / Cooking Time: 14 Mins.

Ingredients:

- » 1 C. honey graham cracker crumbs
- » 2 tbsp. unsalted butter, softened
- » 1 lb. cream cheese, softened
- » ½ C. sugar
- » 2 large eggs

Directions:

1. Line a round baking pan with parchment paper.
2. For crust: in a bowl, add the graham cracker crumbs and butter.
3. Place the crust into the baking dish and press to smooth.
4. Press "Power Button" of Ninja Foodi Air Fry Oven and turn the dial to select the "Air Fry" mode.
5. Press "Time Button" and again turn the dial to set the cooking time to 4 minutes.
6. Now push "Temp Button" and rotate the dial to set the temperature at 350 degrees F.
7. Press "Start/Pause" button to start.
8. When the unit beeps to show that it is preheated, open the lid.
9. Arrange the baking pan of crust into the air fry basket and insert in the oven.
10. When cooking time is complete, open the lid and place the crust aside to cool for about 10 minutes.
11. Meanwhile, in a bowl, add the cream cheese and sugar and whisk until smooth.
12. Now, place the eggs, one at a time and whisk until the mixture becomes creamy.
13. Add the vanilla extract and mix well.
14. Place the cream cheese mixture over the crust evenly.
15. Press "Power Button" of Ninja Foodi Air Fry Oven and turn the dial to select the "Air Fry" mode.
16. Press "Time Button" and again turn the dial to set the cooking time to 10 minutes.
17. Now push "Temp Button" and rotate the dial to set the temperature at 350 degrees F.
18. Press "Start/Pause" button to start.
19. When the unit beeps to show that it is preheated, open the lid.
20. Arrange the baking pan into the air fry basket and insert in the oven.
21. When cooking time is complete, open the lid and place the pan onto a wire rack to cool completely.
22. Refrigerate overnight before serving.
23. Serving Suggestions: Serve with the topping of fresh berries.
24. Variation Tip: Your cream cheese should always be at room temperature.

Nutrition: *Calories: 470 Fat: 33.9g, Sat Fat: 20.6g Carbohydrates: 349g, Fiber: 0.5g Sugar: 22g Protein: 9.4g*

Cheddar Biscuits

Servings: 8 / Cooking Time: 10 Mins.

Ingredients:

- 1/3 C. unbleached all-purpose flour
- 1/8 tsp. cayenne pepper
- 1/8 tsp. smoked paprika
- Pinch of garlic powder
- Salt and freshly ground black pepper, to taste
- ½ C. sharp cheddar cheese, shredded
- 2 tbsp. butter, softened
- Nonstick cooking spray

Directions:

1. In a food processor, add the flour, spices, salt and black pepper and pulse until well combined.
2. Add the cheese and butter and pulse until a smooth dough forms.
3. Place the dough onto a lightly floured surface.
4. Make 16 small equal-sized balls from the dough and press each slightly.
5. Press "Power Button" of Ninja Foodi Digital Air Fry Oven and turn the dial to select "Air Bake" mode.
6. Press "Time Button" and again turn the dial to set the cooking time to 10 minutes.
7. Now push "Temp Button" and rotate the dial to set the temperature at 330 degrees F.
8. Press "Start/Pause" button to start.
9. When the unit beeps to show that it is preheated, open the lid and grease the air fry basket.
10. Arrange the biscuits into the prepared air fry basket and insert in the oven.
11. When cooking time is complete, open the lid and place the basket onto a wire rack for about 10 minutes.
12. Carefully invert the biscuits onto the wire rack to cool completely before serving.
13. Serving Suggestions: Serve these cheddar biscuits with the drizzling of garlic butter.
14. Variation Tip: For flaky layers, use cold butter.

Nutrition: *Calories: 73 Fat: 5.3g Sat Fat: 3.3g Carbohydrates: 4.1g Fiber: 0.2g Sugar: 0.1g Protein: 2.3g*

Glazed Figs

Servings: 4 / Cooking Time: 10 Mins.

Ingredients:

- 4 fresh figs
- 4 tsp. honey
- 2/3 C. Mascarpone cheese, softened
- Pinch of ground cinnamon

Directions:

1. Cut each fig into the quarter, leaving just a little at the base to hold the fruit together.
2. Arrange the figs onto a parchment paper-lined sheet pan and drizzle with honey.
3. Place about 2 tsp. of Mascarpone cheese in the center of each fig and sprinkle with cinnamon.
4. Press "Power Button" of Ninja Foodi Digital Air Fry Oven and turn the dial to select the "Air Broil" mode.
5. Press "Time Button" and again turn the dial to set the cooking time to 10 minutes.
6. Press "Start/Pause" button to start.
7. When the unit beeps to show that it is preheated, open the lid and insert the sheet pan in oven.
8. When cooking time is complete, open the lid and transfer the figs onto a platter.
9. Serve warm.
10. Serving Suggestions: Topping of chopped nuts will add a nice nutty texture.
11. Variation Tip: Select figs that are clean and dry, with smooth, unbroken skin.

Nutrition: *Calories: 141 Fat: 5.5g Sat Fat: 3.5g Carbohydrates: 19.2g Fiber: 1.9g Sugar: 15g Protein: 5.3g*

Red Velvet Cupcakes

Servings: 12 / Cooking Time: 12 Mins.

Ingredients:

For Cupcakes:
- 2 C. refined flour
- ¾ C. icing sugar
- 2 tsp. beet powder
- 1 tsp. cocoa powder
- ¾ C. peanut butter
- 3 eggs
- For Frosting:
- 1 C. butter
- 1 (8-ounce) package cream cheese, softened
- 2 tsp. vanilla extract
- ¼ tsp. salt
- 4½ C. powdered sugar

For Garnishing:
- ½ C. fresh raspberries

Directions:

1. For cupcakes: in a bowl, add all the ingredients and with an electric whisker, whisk until well combined.
2. Place the mixture into silicone cups.
3. Press "Power Button" of Ninja Foodi Digital Air Fry Oven and turn the dial to select "Air Fry" mode.
4. Press "Time Button" and again turn the dial to set the cooking time to 12 minutes.
5. Now push "Temp Button" and rotate the dial to set the temperature at 340 degrees F.
6. Press "Start/Pause" button to start.
7. When the unit beeps to show that it is preheated, open the lid.
8. Arrange the silicone C. into the air fry basket and insert in the oven.
9. When cooking time is complete, open the lid and place the silicone C. onto a wire rack to cool for about 10 minutes.
10. Carefully invert the cupcakes onto the wire rack to completely cool before frosting.
11. For frosting: in a large bowl, mix well butter, cream cheese, vanilla extract, and salt.
12. Add the powdered sugar, one C. at a time, whisking well after each addition.
13. Spread frosting over each cupcake.
14. Garnish with raspberries and serve.
15. Serving Suggestions: Garnishing of sprinkles will add a festive touch in cupcakes.
16. Variation Tip: Measure the ingredients with care.

Nutrition: *Calories: 599, Fat: 31.5g, Sat Fat: 16g Carbohydrates: 73.2g, Fiber: 2g Sugar: 53.4g, Protein: 9.3g*

Air Fryer Lumpia

Servings: 16 / Cooking Time: 20 Mins.

Ingredients:

- 1 oz. Italian hot sausage links
- ½ C. carrots, chopped
- ½ C. onions, diced and sliced
- ½ C. water chestnut, chopped
- 2 garlic cloves, minced

Directions:

1. Take out casing from the sausage. Cook on medium heat for 4-5 minutes. It should turn light brown.
2. Add the onions, water chestnut, and carrot.
3. Cook while stirring. The onions should become translucent and soft.
4. Now include the garlic. Cook for 1 more minute. Season with salt.
5. Keep stirring to combine well. Take out from the heat.
6. Keep a spring roll wrapper and at its center, place one-fourth of the filling.
7. Fold the bottom corner. Tuck the sides in, forming a roll.
8. Moisten the edges using water. Apply avocado oil spray.
9. Preheat your air fryer to 198 degrees C or 390 degrees F.
10. Keep the rolls in the fryer basket and cook for 4 minutes.
11. Flip once and cook for 4 more minutes. The skins should get crispy.

Nutrition: *Calories 111, Carbohydrates 7g, Cholesterol 12mg, Total Fat 7g, Protein 5g, Sugar 1g, Fiber 1g, Sodium 471mg*

Gluten-free Cherry Crumble

Servings: 4 / Cooking Time: 25 Mins.

Ingredients:

- 3 C. pitted cherries
- 2 tsp. of lemon juice
- 1/3 C. butter
- 1 C. gluten-free all-purpose baking flour
- 1 tsp. vanilla powder
- 10 tbsp. of white sugar

Directions:

1. Cube the butter and refrigerate for about 15 minutes. It should get firm.
2. Preheat your air fryer to 165 degrees C or 325 degrees F.
3. Bring together the pitted cherries, lemon juice, and 2 tbsp. of sugar in your bowl. Mix well.
4. Pour the cherry mix into a baking dish.
5. Now mix 6 tbsp. of sugar and flour in a bowl.
6. Use your fingers to cut in the butter. Particles should be pea-size.
7. Keep them over the cherries. Press down lightly.
8. Stir in the vanilla powder and 2 tbsp. of sugar in your bowl.
9. Dust the sugar topping over flour and cherries.
10. Transfer to your air fryer and bake.
11. Leave it inside for 10 minutes once the baking is done.
12. Set aside for 5 minutes to cool.

Nutrition: Calories 576, Carbohydrates 76g, Cholesterol 41mg, Total Fat 28g, Protein 5g, Sugar 49g, Fiber 6g, Sodium 109mg

Apple Fritters

Servings: 4 / Cooking Time: 10 Mins.

Ingredients:

- 1 apple – cored, peeled, and chopped
- 1 C. all-purpose flour
- 1 egg
- ½ C. milk
- 1-1/2 tsp. of baking powder
- 2 tbsp. white sugar

Directions:

1. Preheat your air fryer to 175 degrees C or 350 degrees F.
2. Keep parchment paper at the bottom of your fryer.
3. Apply cooking spray.
4. Mix together ¼ C. sugar, flour, baking powder, egg, milk, and salt in a bowl.
5. Combine well by stirring.
6. Sprinkle 2 tbsp. of sugar on the apples. Coat well.
7. Combine the apples into your flour mixture.
8. Use a cookie scoop and drop the fritters with it to the air fryer basket's bottom.
9. Now air fry for 5 minutes.
10. Flip the fritters once and fry for another 3 minutes. They should be golden.

Nutrition: Calories 307, Carbohydrates 65g, Cholesterol 48mg, Total Fat 3g, Protein 5g, Sugar 39g, Fiber 2g, Sodium 248mg

Banana Split

Servings: 8 / Cooking Time: 14 Mins.

Ingredients:

- 3 tbsp. coconut oil
- 1 C. panko breadcrumbs
- ½ C. corn flour
- 2 eggs
- 4 bananas, peeled and halved lengthwise
- 3 tbsp. sugar
- ¼ tsp. ground cinnamon
- 2 tbsp. walnuts, chopped

Directions:

1. In a medium skillet, melt the coconut oil over medium heat and cook breadcrumbs for about 3-4 minutes or until golden browned and crumbled, stirring continuously.
2. Transfer the breadcrumbs into a shallow bowl and set aside to cool.
3. In a second bowl, place the corn flour.
4. In a third bowl, whisk the eggs.
5. Coat the banana slices with flour and then, dip into eggs and finally, coat with the breadcrumbs evenly.
6. In a small bowl, mix together the sugar and cinnamon.
7. Press "Power Button" of Ninja Foodi Digital Air Fry Oven and turn the dial to select "Air Fry" mode.
8. Press "Time Button" and again turn the dial to set the cooking time to 10 minutes.
9. Now push "Temp Button" and rotate the dial to set the temperature at 280 degrees F.
10. Press "Start/Pause" button to start.
11. When the unit beeps to show that it is preheated, open the lid.
12. Arrange the banana slices into the air fry basket and sprinkle with cinnamon sugar.
13. Insert the basket in the oven.
14. When cooking time is complete, open the lid and transfer the banana slices onto plates to cool slightly
15. Sprinkle with chopped walnuts and serve.
16. Serving Suggestions: Serve with a scoop of strawberry ice cream.
17. Variation Tip: Pecans will be an excellent substitute for walnuts.

Nutrition: *Calories: 216 Fat: 8.8g Sat Fat: 5.3g Carbohydrates: 26g Fiber: 2.3g Sugar: 11.9g Protein: 3.4g*

Spicy Chickpeas

Servings: 4 / Cooking Time: 10 Mins.

Ingredients:

- 1 (15-ounce) can chickpeas, rinsed and drained
- 1 tbsp. olive oil
- ½ tsp. cayenne pepper
- ½ tsp. smoked paprika
- ½ tsp. ground cumin
- 1/8 tsp. ground cinnamon
- Salt, to taste

Directions:

1. In a bowl, add all the ingredients and toss to coat well.
2. Press "Power Button" of Ninja Foodi Digital Air Fry Oven and turn the dial to select "Air Fry" mode.
3. Press "Time Button" and again turn the dial to set the cooking time to 10 minutes.
4. Now push "Temp Button" and rotate the dial to set the temperature at 390 degrees F.
5. Press "Start/Pause" button to start.
6. When the unit beeps to show that it is preheated, open the lid.
7. Arrange the chickpeas into the air fry basket and insert in the oven.
8. When cooking time is complete, open the lid and transfer the chickpeas into a bowl.
9. Serve warm.
10. Serving Suggestions: These roasted chickpeas can also be used as a topping of potato soup.
11. Variation Tip: You can adjust the ratio of spices according to your taste.

Nutrition: *Calories: 146 Fat: 4.5g Sat Fat: 0.5g Carbohydrates: 18.8g Fiber: 4.6g Sugar: 0.1g Protein: 6.3g*

POULTRY RECIPES

Turkish Chicken Kebab

Servings: 4 / Cooking Time: 15 Mins.

Ingredients:

- » 1 oz. Chicken thighs, boneless and skinless
- » ¼ C. Greek yogurt, plain
- » 1 tbsp. tomato paste
- » 1 tbsp. vegetable oil
- » ½ tsp. cinnamon, ground

Directions:

1. Stir together the tomato paste, Greek yogurt, oil, cinnamon, salt, and pepper in a bowl. The spices should blend well into the yogurt.
2. Cut the chicken into 4 pieces.
3. Now include your chicken pieces into the mixture. Make sure that the chicken is coated well with the mixture.
4. Refrigerate for 30 minutes' minimum.
5. Take out chicken from your marinade.
6. Keep in your air fryer basket in a single layer.
7. Set your fryer to 370 degrees F. Cook the chicken pieces for 8 minutes.
8. Flip over and cook for another 4 minutes.

Nutrition: *Calories 375, Carbohydrates 4g, Cholesterol 112mg, Total Fat 31g, Protein 20g, Sugar 1g, Fiber 1g*

Spiced Chicken Thighs

Servings: 4 / Cooking Time: 20 Mins.

Ingredients:

- 1 tsp. ground cumin
- 1 tsp. garlic powder
- ½ tsp. smoked paprika
- ½ tsp. ground coriander
- Salt and ground black pepper, as required
- 4 (5-ounce) chicken thighs

Directions:

1. In a large bowl, add the spices, salt and black pepper and mix well.
2. Coat the chicken thighs with oil and then rub with spice mixture.
3. Arrange the chicken thighs onto the sheet pan.
4. Press "Power Button" of Ninja Foodi Digital Air Fry Oven and turn the dial to select "Air Fry" mode.
5. Press "Time Button" and again turn the dial to set the cooking time to 20 minutes.
6. Now push "Temp Button" and rotate the dial to set the temperature at 400 degrees F.
7. Press "Start/Pause" button to start.
8. When the unit beeps to show that it is preheated, open the lid and insert the sheet pan in the oven.
9. Flip the chicken thighs once halfway through.
10. When cooking time is complete, open the lid and transfer the chicken thighs onto serving plates.
11. Serve hot.
12. Serving Suggestions: Serve with a fresh green salad.
13. Variation Tip: Adjust the ratio of spices according to your spice tolerance.

Nutrition: Calories: 334 Fat: 17.7g Sat Fat: 3.9g Carbohydrates: 0.9g Fiber: 0.2g Sugar: 0.2g Protein: 41.3g

Air Fryer Egg Rolls

Servings: 16 / Cooking Time: 15 Mins.

Ingredients:

- 1 pack of egg roll wrappers
- 2 C. corn, thawed
- 1 can spinach, drained
- 1 can black beans, drained and rinsed
- 1 C. cheddar cheese, shredded

Directions:

1. Mix the corn, spinach, beans, Cheddar cheese, salt, and pepper in a bowl. This is for the filling.
2. Keep an egg roll wrapper.
3. Moisten lightly all the edges with your finger.
4. Keep a fourth of the filling at the wrapper's center.
5. Now fold a corner over the filling. Tuck the sides in to create a roll.
6. Repeat this process with the other wrappers.
7. Apply cooking spray on the egg rolls.
8. Preheat your air fryer at 199 degrees C or 390 degrees F.
9. Keep your egg rolls in its basket. They should not touch each other.
10. Fry for 7 minutes. Flip and cook for another 4 minutes.

Nutrition: Calories 260, Carbohydrates 27g, Cholesterol 25mg, Total Fat 12g, Protein 11g, Sugar 1g, Fiber 4g, Sodium 628mg

Thyme Duck Breast

Servings: 2 / Cooking Time: 20 Mins.

Ingredients:

- 1 C. beer
- 1 tbsp. olive oil
- 1 tsp. mustard
- 1 tbsp. fresh thyme, chopped
- Salt and freshly ground black pepper, to taste
- 1 (10½-ounce) duck breast

Directions:

1. In a bowl, add the beer, oil, mustard, thyme, salt, and black pepper and mix well
2. Add the duck breast and coat with marinade generously.
3. Cover and refrigerate for about 4 hours.
4. Arrange the duck breast onto the greased sheet pan.
5. Press "Power Button" of Ninja Foodi Digital Air Fry Oven and turn the dial to select "Air Fry" mode.
6. Press "Time Button" and again turn the dial to set the cooking time to 20 minutes.
7. Now push "Temp Button" and rotate the dial to set the temperature at 390 degrees F.
8. Press "Start/Pause" button to start.
9. When the unit beeps to show that it is preheated, open the lid and insert the sheet pan in the oven.
10. Flip the duck breast once halfway through.
11. When cooking time is complete, open the lid and place the duck breast onto a cutting board for about 5 minutes before slicing.
12. With a sharp knife, cut the duck breast into desired size slices and serve.
13. Serving Suggestions: Duck meat goes really well with caramelized onions or balsamic reduction.
14. Variation Tip: Look for a plump, firm breast for best flav

Nutrition: Calories: 315 Fat: 13.5g Sat Fat: 1.1g Carbohydrates: 5.7g Fiber: 0.7g Sugar: 0.1g Protein: 33.8g

Herbed Turkey Breast

Servings: 6 / Cooking Time: 40 Mins.

Ingredients:

- ¼ C. unsalted butter, softened
- 2 tbsp. fresh rosemary, chopped
- 2 tbsp. fresh thyme, chopped
- 2 tbsp. fresh sage, chopped
- 2 tbsp. fresh parsley, chopped
- Salt and freshly ground black pepper, to taste
- 1 (4-pound) bone-in, skin-on turkey breast
- 2 tbsp. olive oil

Directions:

1. In a bowl, add the butter, herbs, salt and black pepper and mix well.
2. Rub the herb mixture under skin evenly.
3. Coat the outside of turkey breast with oil.
4. Place the turkey breast into the greased baking pan.
5. Press "Power Button" of Ninja Foodi Digital Air Fry Oven and turn the dial to select "Air Bake" mode.
6. Press "Time Button" and again turn the dial to set the cooking time to 40 minutes.
7. Now push "Temp Button" and rotate the dial to set the temperature at 350 degrees F.
8. Press "Start/Pause" button to start.
9. When the unit beeps to show that it is preheated, open the lid and insert baking pan in the oven.
10. When cooking time is complete, open the lid and place the turkey breast onto a platter for about 5-10 minutes before slicing.
11. With a sharp knife, cut the turkey breast into desired sized slices and serve.
12. Serving Suggestions: Roasted potatoes will accompany this turkey breast nicely.
13. Variation Tip: Use unsalted butter.

Nutrition: Calories: 333 Fat: 37g Sat Fat: 12.4g Carbohydrates: 1.8g Fiber: 1.1g Sugar: 0.1g Protein: 65.1g

Marinated Chicken Thighs

Servings: 4 / Cooking Time: 30 Mins.

Ingredients:

- 4 (6-ounce) bone-in, skin-on chicken thighs
- Salt and freshly ground black pepper, to taste
- ½ C. Italian salad dressing
- 1 tsp. onion powder
- 1 tsp. garlic powder

Directions:

1. Season the chicken thighs with salt and black pepper evenly.
2. In a large bowl, add the chicken thighs and dressing and mix well.
3. Cover the bowl and refrigerate to marinate overnight.
4. Remove the chicken breast from the bowl and place onto a plate.
5. Sprinkle the chicken thighs with onion powder and garlic powder.
6. Press "Power Button" of Ninja Foodi Digital Air Fry Oven and turn the dial to select "Air Fry" mode.
7. Press "Time Button" and again turn the dial to set the cooking time to 30 minutes.
8. Now push "Temp Button" and rotate the dial to set the temperature at 360 degrees F.
9. Press "Start/Pause" button to start.
10. When the unit beeps to show that it is preheated, open the lid and grease the air fry basket.
11. Arrange the chicken thighs into the prepared basket and insert in the oven.
12. After 15 minutes of cooking, flip the chicken thighs once.
13. When cooking time is complete, open the lid and transfer the chicken thighs onto serving plates.
14. Serve hot.
15. Serving Suggestions: Enjoy with honey glazed baby carrots.
16. Variation Tip: Select the chicken thighs with a pinkish hue.

Nutrition: *Calories: 413 Fat: 21g Sat Fat: 4.8g Carbohydrates: 4.1g Fiber: 0.1g Sugar: 2.8g Protein: 49.5g*

Blackened Chicken Breast

Servings: 2 / Cooking Time: 20 Mins.

Ingredients:

- 2 chicken breast halves, skinless and boneless
- 1 tsp. thyme, ground
- 2 tsp. of paprika
- 2 tsp. vegetable oil
- ½ tsp. onion powder

Directions:

1. Combine the thyme, paprika, onion powder, and salt together in your bowl.
2. Transfer the spice mix to a flat plate.
3. Rub vegetable oil on the chicken breast. Coat fully.
4. Roll the chicken pieces in the spice mixture. Press down, ensuring that all sides have the spice mix.
5. Keep aside for 5 minutes.
6. In the meantime, preheat your air fryer to 175 degrees C or 360 degrees F.
7. Keep the chicken in the air fryer basket. Cook for 8 minutes.
8. Flip once and cook for another 7 minutes.
9. Transfer the breasts to a serving plate. Serve after 5 minutes.

Nutrition: Calories 427, Carbohydrates 3g, Cholesterol 198mg, Total Fat 11g, Protein 79g, Sugar 1g, Fiber 2g, Sodium 516mg

Roasted Cornish Game Hen

Servings: 4 / Cooking Time: 16 Mins.

Ingredients:

- ¼ C. olive oil
- 1 tsp. fresh rosemary, chopped
- 1 tsp. fresh thyme, chopped
- 1 tsp. fresh lemon zest, finely grated
- ¼ tsp. sugar
- ¼ tsp. red pepper flakes, crushed
- Salt and freshly ground black pepper, to taste
- 2 lb. Cornish game hen, backbone removed and halved

Directions:

1. In a bowl, mix together oil, herbs, lemon zest, sugar, and spices.
2. Add the hen portions and coat with the marinade generously.
3. Cover and refrigerate for about 24 hours.
4. In a strainer, place the hen portions and set aside to drain any liquid.
5. Press "Power Button" of Ninja Foodi Digital Air Fry Oven and turn the dial to select "Air Fry" mode.
6. Press "Time Button" and again turn the dial to set the cooking time to 16 minutes.
7. Now push "Temp Button" and rotate the dial to set the temperature at 390 degrees F.
8. Press "Start/Pause" button to start.
9. When the unit beeps to show that it is preheated, open the lid and grease the air fry basket.
10. Arrange the hen portions into the prepared basket and insert in the oven.
11. When cooking time is complete, open the lid and transfer the hen portions onto a platter.
12. Cut each portion in half and serve.
13. Serving Suggestions: Serve with dinner rolls.
14. Variation Tip: Place the hens in the basket, breast side up.

Nutrition: *Calories: 557 Fat: 45.1g Sat Fat: 1.8g Carbohydrates: 0.8g Fiber: 0.3g Sugar: 0.3g Protein: 38.5g*

MEAT RECIPES

Mushrooms With Steak

Servings: 4 / Cooking Time: 10 Mins.

Ingredients:

- » 1 oz. sirloin beef steak, cut into small 1-inch cubes
- » ¼ C. Worcestershire sauce
- » 8 oz. sliced button mushrooms
- » 1 tbsp. of olive oil
- » 1 tsp. chili flakes, crushed

Directions:

1. Combine the mushrooms, steak, olive oil Worcestershire sauce, and chili flakes in your bowl.
2. Keep it refrigerated for 4 hours minimum.
3. Take out 30 minutes before cooking.
4. Preheat your oven to 200 degrees C or 400 degrees F.
5. Drain out the marinade from your steak mixture.
6. Now keep the mushrooms and steak in the air fryer basket.
7. Cook for 5 minutes in the air fryer.
8. Toss and then cook for another 5 minutes.
9. Transfer the mushrooms and steak to a serving plate.

Nutrition: Calories 261, Carbohydrates 6g, Cholesterol 60mg, Total Fat 17g, Protein 21g, Sugar 3g, Fiber 0.9g, Sodium 213mg

Pork Skewers With Mango Salsa & Black Bean

Servings: 4 / Cooking Time: 10 Mins.

Ingredients:

- 1 lb. pork tenderloin, cut into small cubes
- ½ can black beans, rinsed and drained
- 1 mango, peeled, seeded, and chopped
- 4-1/2 tsp. of onion powder
- 4-1/2 tsp. thyme, crushed
- 1 tbsp. vegetable oil
- ¼ tsp. cloves, ground

Directions:

1. Stir in the thyme, onion powder, salt, and cloves in a bowl to create the seasoning mixture.
2. Keep a tbsp. of this for the pork. Transfer the remaining to an airtight container for later.
3. Preheat your air fryer to 175 degrees C or 350 degrees F.
4. Thread the chunks of pork into the skewers.
5. Brush oil on the pork. Sprinkle the seasoning mix on all sides.
6. Keep in your air fryer basket.
7. Cook for 5 minutes.
8. Mash one-third of the mango in your bowl in the meantime.
9. Stir the remaining mango in, and also salt, pepper, and black beans.
10. Serve the salsa with the pork skewers.

Nutrition: Calories 372, Carbohydrates 35g, Cholesterol 49mg, Total Fat 16g, Fiber 7g, Protein 22g, Sugar 18g, Sodium 1268mg

Braised Lamb Shanks

Servings: 4 / Cooking Time: 2 Hours, 30 Mins.

Ingredients:

- 4 lamb shanks
- 4 crushed garlic cloves
- 2 tbsp. of olive oil
- 3 C. of beef broth
- 2 tbsp. balsamic vinegar

Directions:

1. Rub pepper and salt on your lamb shanks. Keep in the baking pan.
2. Rub the smashed garlic on the lamb well.
3. Now cut the shanks with olive oil.
4. Keep underneath your lamb.
5. Keep the pan into the rack.
6. Roast for 20 minutes at 425 degrees F. Change to low for 2 hours at 250 F.
7. Add vinegar and 2 C. of broth.
8. Including the remaining broth after the 1st hour.

Nutrition: Calories 453, Carbohydrates 6g, Cholesterol 121mg, Total Fat 37g, Protein 24g, Fiber 2g, Sodium 578mg

Buttered Rib Eye Steak

Servings: 3 / Cooking Time: 14 Mins.

Ingredients:

- 2 (8-ounce) rib eye steaks
- 2 tbsp. butter, melted
- Salt and ground black pepper, as required

Directions:

1. Coat the steak with butter and then, sprinkle with salt and black pepper evenly.
2. Press "Power Button" of Ninja Foodi Digital Air Fry Oven and turn the dial to select the "Air Roast" mode.
3. Press the Time button and again turn the dial to set the cooking time to 14 minutes.
4. Now push the Temp button and rotate the dial to set the temperature at 400 degrees F.
5. Press "Start/Pause" button to start.
6. When the unit beeps to show that it is preheated, open the lid and grease "Air Fry Basket".
7. Arrange the steaks into "Air Fry Basket" and insert in the oven.
8. Remove from the oven and place steaks onto a platter for about 5 minutes.
9. Cut each steak into desired size slices and serve.

Nutrition: Calories 388 Total Fat 23.7 g Saturated Fat 110.2 g Cholesterol 154 mg Sodium 278 mg Total Carbs 0 g Fiber 0 g Sugar 0 g Protein 41 g

Beef Sirloin Roast

Servings: 8 / Cooking Time: 50 Mins.

Ingredients:

- 1 tbsp. smoked paprika
- 1 tsp. ground cumin
- 1 tsp. garlic powder
- Salt and freshly ground black pepper, to taste
- 2½ lb. sirloin roast

Directions:

1. In a bowl, mix together the spices, salt and black pepper.
2. Rub the roast with spice mixture generously.
3. Place the sirloin roast into the greased baking pan.
4. Press "Power Button" of Ninja Foodi Digital Air Fry Oven and turn the dial to select "Air Roast" mode.
5. Press "Time Button" and again turn the dial to set the cooking time to 50 minutes.
6. Now push "Temp Button" and rotate the dial to set the temperature at 350 degrees F.
7. Press "Start/Pause" button to start.
8. When the unit beeps to show that it is preheated, open the lid and insert baking pan in the oven.
9. When cooking time is complete, open the lid and place the roast onto a platter for about 10 minutes before slicing.
10. With a sharp knife, cut the beef roast into desired sized slices and serve.
11. Serving Suggestions: Serve this roast with a topping of herbed butter.
12. Variation Tip: Rub the seasoning over the roast with your fingers, covering the entire exterior with an even layer.

Nutrition: Calories: 260 Fat: 11.9g Sat Fat: 4.4g Carbohydrates: 0.4g Fiber: 0.1g Sugar: 0.1g Protein: 38g

Air-fried Meatloaf

Servings: 4 / Cooking Time: 45 Mins.

Ingredients:

- 8 oz. pork, ground
- 8 oz. veal, ground
- 1 large egg
- ¼ C. bread crumbs
- 1.4 C. cilantro, chopped
- 1 tsp. of olive oil
- 2 tsp. chipotle chili sauce

Directions:

1. Preheat your air fryer to 200 degrees C or 400 degrees F.
2. Bring together the veal and pork in a baking dish. Make sure that it goes into your air fryer basket.
3. Create a well. Now add the cilantro, egg, bread crumbs, salt, and pepper.
4. Use your hands to mix well and create a loaf.
5. Combine the olive oil and chipotle chili sauce in a bowl. Whisk well.
6. Keep it aside.
7. Cook the meatloaf in your air fryer. Take it out and add the juicy mix.
8. Bring back the meatloaf to the fryer. Bake for 7 minutes.
9. Turn the fryer off. Allow the meatloaf to rest for 6 minutes inside.
10. Take it out and let it rest for 5 more minutes.
11. Slice before serving.

Nutrition: *Calories 311, Carbohydrates 13g, Cholesterol 123mg, Total Fat 19g, Fiber 0.7g, Protein 22g, Sugar 8g, Sodium 536mg*

Pork Stuffed Bell Peppers

Servings: 4 / Cooking Time: 1 Hour 10 Mins.

Ingredients:

- 4 medium green bell peppers
- 2/3-pound ground pork
- 2 C. cooked white rice
- 1½ C. marinara sauce, divided
- 1 tsp. Worcestershire sauce
- 1 tsp. Italian seasoning
- Salt and ground black pepper, as required
- ½ C. mozzarella cheese, shredded

Directions:

1. Cut the tops from bell peppers and then carefully remove the seeds.
2. Heat a large skillet over medium heat and cook the pork for bout 6-8 minutes, breaking into crumbles.
3. Add the rice, ¾ C. of marinara sauce, Worcestershire sauce, Italian seasoning, salt and black pepper and stir to combine.
4. Remove from the heat.
5. Arrange the bell peppers into the greased baking pan.
6. Carefully, stuff each bell pepper with the pork mixture and top each with the remaining sauce.
7. Press "Power Button" of Ninja Foodi Digital Air Fry Oven and turn the dial to select the "Air Bake" mode.
8. Press the Time button and again turn the dial to set the cooking time to 60 minutes.
9. Now push the Temp button and rotate the dial to set the temperature at 350 degrees F.
10. Press "Start/Pause" button to start.
11. When the unit beeps to show that it is preheated, open the lid.
12. Insert the baking pan in oven.
13. After 50 minutes of cooking, top each bell pepper with cheese.
14. Serve warm.

Nutrition: Calories 580 Total Fat 7.1 g Saturated Fat 2.2 g Cholesterol 60 mg Sodium 509 mg Total Carbs 96.4 g Fiber 5.2 g Sugar 14.8 g Protein 30.3 g

Glazed Pork Tenderloin

Servings: 3 / Cooking Time: 20 Mins.

Ingredients:

- 2 tbsp. Sriracha
- 2 tbsp. maple syrup
- ¼ tsp. red pepper flakes, crushed
- Salt, to taste
- 1 lb. pork tenderloin

Directions:

1. In a small bowl, add the Sriracha, maple syrup, red pepper flakes and salt and mix well.
2. Brush the pork tenderloin with mixture evenly.
3. Press "Power Button" of Ninja Foodi Digital Air Fry Oven and turn the dial to select "Air Fry" mode.
4. Press "Time Button" and again turn the dial to set the cooking time to 20 minutes.
5. Now push "Temp Button" and rotate the dial to set the temperature at 350 degrees F.
6. Press "Start/Pause" button to start.
7. When the unit beeps to show that it is preheated, open the lid and grease air fry basket.
8. Arrange the pork tenderloin into the air fry basket and insert in the oven.
9. When cooking time is complete, open the lid and place the pork tenderloin onto a platter for about 10 minutes before slicing.
10. With a sharp knife, cut the roast into desired sized slices and serve.
11. Serving Suggestions: Fig and arugula salad will brighten the taste of tenderloin.
12. Variation Tip: The addition of dried herbs will add a delish touch in pork tenderloin.

Nutrition: *Calories: 261 Fat: 5.4g Sat Fat: 1.8g Carbohydrates: 11g Fiber: 0g Sugar: 8g Protein: 39.6g*

FISH & SEAFOOD RECIPES

Buttered Salmon

Servings: 2 / Cooking Time: 10 Mins.

Ingredients:

- 2 (6-ounce) salmon fillets
- Salt and freshly ground black pepper, to taste
- 1 tbsp. butter, melted

Directions:

1. Season each salmon fillet with salt and black pepper and then, coat with the butter.
2. Press "Power Button" of Ninja Foodi Digital Air Fry Oven and turn the dial to select "Air Fry" mode.
3. Press "Time Button" and again turn the dial to set the cooking time to 10 minutes.
4. Now push "Temp Button" and rotate the dial to set the temperature at 360 degrees F.
5. Press "Start/Pause" button to start.
6. When the unit beeps to show that it is preheated, open the lid and grease the air fry basket.
7. Arrange the salmon fillets into the prepared air fry basket and insert in the oven.
8. When cooking time is complete, open the lid and transfer the salmon fillets onto serving plates.
9. Serve hot.
10. Serving Suggestions: Enjoy with roasted parsnip puree.
11. Variation Tip: Salmon should look bright and shiny.

Nutrition: *Calories: 276 Fat: 16.3g Sat Fat: 5.2g Carbohydrates: 0g Fiber: 0g Sugar: 0g Protein: 33.1g*

Seasoned Catfish

Servings: 4 / Cooking Time: 23 Mins.

Ingredients:

» 4 (4-ounce) catfish fillets
» 2 tbsp. Italian seasoning
» Salt and freshly ground black pepper, to taste
» 1 tbsp. olive oil
» 1 tbsp. fresh parsley, chopped

Directions:

1. Rub the fish fillets with seasoning, salt and black pepper generously and then coat with oil.
2. Press "Power Button" of Ninja Foodi Digital Air Fry Oven and turn the dial to select "Air Fry" mode.
3. Press "Time Button" and again turn the dial to set the cooking time to 20 minutes.
4. Now push "Temp Button" and rotate the dial to set the temperature at 400 degrees F.
5. Press "Start/Pause" button to start.
6. When the unit beeps to show that it is preheated, open the lid and grease the air fry basket.
7. Arrange the fish fillets into the prepared air fry basket and insert in the oven.
8. Flip the fish fillets once halfway through.
9. When cooking time is complete, open the lid and transfer the fillets onto serving plates.
10. Serve hot with the garnishing of parsley.
11. Serving Suggestions: Quinoa salad will be a great choice for serving.
12. Variation Tip: Season the fish according to your choice.

Nutrition: *Calories: 205 Fat: 14.2g Sat Fat: 2.4g Carbohydrates: 0.8g Fiber: 0g Sugar: 0.6g Protein: 17.7g*

Lemony Shrimp

Servings: 3 / Cooking Time: 8 Mins.

Ingredients:

- » 2 tbsp. fresh lemon juice
- » 1 tbsp. olive oil
- » 1 tsp. lemon pepper
- » ¼ tsp. paprika
- » ¼ tsp. garlic powder
- » 12 oz. medium shrimp, peeled and deveined

Directions:

1. In a large bowl, add all the ingredients except the shrimp and mix until well combined.
2. Add the shrimp and toss to coat well.
3. Arrange the shrimps onto a sheet pan.
4. Press "Power Button" of Ninja Foodi Digital Air Fry Oven and turn the dial to select "Air Fry" mode.
5. Press "Time Button" and again turn the dial to set the cooking time to 8 minutes.
6. Now push "Temp Button" and rotate the dial to set the temperature at 400 degrees F.
7. Press "Start/Pause" button to start.
8. When the unit beeps to show that it is preheated, open the lid and insert the sheet pan in the oven.
9. When cooking time is complete, open the lid and transfer the shrimp onto serving plates.
10. Serve hot.
11. Serving Suggestions: Serve with scalloped potatoes.
12. Variation Tip: Avoid shrimp that smell like ammonia.

Nutrition: *Calories: 164 Fat: 6.1g Sat Fat: 0.8g Carbohydrates: 0.9g Fiber: 0.3g Sugar: 0.3g Protein: 24.5g*

Spiced Tilapia

Servings: 2 / Cooking Time: 12 Mins.

Ingredients:

- ¼ tsp. garlic powder
- ¼ tsp. onion powder
- ¼ tsp. ground cumin
- Salt and ground black pepper, as required
- 2 (6-ounce) tilapia fillets
- 1 tbsp. butter, melted

Directions:

1. In a small bowl, mix together the spices, salt and black pepper.
2. Coat the tilapia fillets with oil and then rub with spice mixture.
3. Press "Power Button" of Ninja Foodi Digital Air Fry Oven and turn the dial to select the "Air Fry" mode.
4. Press the Time button and again turn the dial to set the cooking time to 12 minutes.
5. Now push the Temp button and rotate the dial to set the temperature at 360 degrees F.
6. Press "Start/Pause" button to start.
7. When the unit beeps to show that it is preheated, open the lid.
8. Arrange the tilapia fillets over the greased "Wire Rack" and insert in the oven.
9. Flip the tilapia fillets once halfway through.
10. Serve hot.

Nutrition: *Calories 194 Total Fat 7.4 g Saturated Fat 4.3 g Cholesterol 98 mg Sodium 179 mg Total Carbs 0.6 g Fiber 0.1 g Sugar 0.2 g Protein 31.8 g*

Zesty Fish Fillets

Servings: 4 / Cooking Time: 12 Mins.

Ingredients:

- 4 fillets of salmon or tilapia
- 2-1/2 tsp. vegetable oil
- ¾ C. crushed cornflakes or bread crumbs
- 2 eggs, beaten
- 1 packet dry dressing mix

Directions:

1. Preheat the air fryer to 180° C.
2. Mix the dressing mix and the breadcrumbs together.
3. Pour the oil. Stir until you see the mix getting crumbly and loose.
4. Now dip your fish fillets into the egg. Remove the excess.
5. Dip your fillets into the crumb mix. Coat evenly.
6. Transfer to the fryer carefully.
7. Cook for 10 minutes. Take out and serve.
8. You can also add some lemon wedges on your fish.

Nutrition: *Calories 382, Carbohydrates 8g, Cholesterol 166mg, Total Fat 22g, Protein 38g, Sodium 220mg, Calcium 50mg*

Cod Parcel

Servings: 2 / Cooking Time: 15 Mins.

Ingredients:

- 2 tbsp. butter, melted
- 1 tbsp. fresh lemon juice
- ½ tsp. dried tarragon
- Salt and freshly ground black pepper, to taste
- ½ C. red bell peppers, seeded and thinly sliced
- ½ C. carrots, peeled and julienned
- ½ C. fennel bulbs, julienned
- 2 (5-ounce) frozen cod fillets, thawed
- 1 tbsp. olive oil

Directions:

1. In a large bowl, mix together the butter, lemon juice, tarragon, salt, and black pepper.
2. Add the bell pepper, carrot, and fennel bulb and generously coat with the mixture.
3. Arrange 2 large parchment squares onto a smooth surface.
4. Coat the cod fillets with oil and then sprinkle evenly with salt and black pepper.
5. Arrange 1 cod fillet onto each parchment square and top each evenly with the vegetables.
6. Top with any remaining sauce from the bowl.
7. Fold the parchment paper and crimp the sides to secure fish and vegetables.
8. Press "Power Button" of Ninja Foodi Digital Air Fry Oven and turn the dial to select "Air Fry" mode.
9. Press "Time Button" and again turn the dial to set the cooking time to 15 minutes.
10. Now push "Temp Button" and rotate the dial to set the temperature at 350 degrees F.
11. Press "Start/Pause" button to start.
12. When the unit beeps to show that it is preheated, open the lid.
13. Arrange the cod parcels into the air fry basket and insert in the oven.
14. When cooking time is complete, open the lid and transfer the cod parcels onto serving plates.
15. Carefully open the parcels and serve hot.
16. Serving Suggestions: Serve with the drizzling of lime juice.
17. Variation Tip: You can use veggies of your choice.

Nutrition: Calories: 306 Fat: 20g Sat Fat: 8.4g Carbohydrates: 6.8g Fiber: 1.8g Sugar: 3g Protein: 26.3g

Ranch Tilapia

Servings: 4 / Cooking Time: 13 Mins.

Ingredients:

- ¾ C. cornflakes, crushed
- 1 (1-ounce) packet dry ranch-style dressing mix
- 2½ tbsp. vegetable oil
- 2 eggs
- 4 (6-ounce) tilapia fillets

Directions:

1. In a shallow bowl, crack the eggs and beat slightly.
2. In another bowl, add the cornflakes, ranch dressing, and oil and mix until a crumbly mixture forms.
3. Dip the fish fillets into egg and then, coat with the breadcrumbs mixture.
4. Press "Power Button" of Ninja Foodi Digital Air Fry Oven and turn the dial to select "Air Fry" mode.
5. Press "Time Button" and again turn the dial to set the cooking time to 13 minutes.
6. Now push "Temp Button" and rotate the dial to set the temperature at 356 degrees F.
7. Press "Start/Pause" button to start.
8. When the unit beeps to show that it is preheated, open the lid and grease the air fry basket.
9. Arrange the tilapia fillets into the prepared air fry basket and insert in the oven. When cooking time is complete, open the lid and transfer the fillets onto serving plates.
10. Serve hot.
11. Serving Suggestions: Serve tilapia with lemon butter.
12. Variation Tip: The skin should be removed, either before cooking or before serving.

Nutrition: *Calories: 267 Fat: 12.2g Sat Fat: 3g Carbohydrates: 5.1g Fiber: 0.2g Sugar: 0.9g Protein: 34.9g*

Pesto Salmon

Servings: 4 / Cooking Time: 15 Mins.

Ingredients:

- 1¼ lb. salmon fillet, cut into 4 fillets
- 2 tbsp. white wine
- 1 tbsp. fresh lemon juice
- 2 tbsp. pesto, thawed
- 2 tbsp. pine nuts, toasted

Directions:

1. Arrange the salmon fillets onto q foil-lined baking pan, skin-side down.
2. Drizzle the salmon fillets with wine and lemon juice.
3. Set aside for about 15 minutes.
4. Spread pesto over each salmon fillet evenly.
5. Press "Power Button" of Ninja Foodi Digital Air Fry Oven and turn the dial to select the "Air Broil" mode.
6. Press the Time button and again turn the dial to set the cooking time to 15 minutes.
7. Press "Start/Pause" button to start.
8. When the unit beeps to show that it is preheated, open the lid.
9. Insert the baking pan in oven.
10. Garnish with toasted pine nuts and serve.

Nutrition: Calories 257 Total Fat 15 g Saturated Fat 2.1 g Cholesterol 64 mg Sodium 111 mg Total Carbs 1.3 g Fiber 0.3 g Sugar 0.8 g Protein 28.9 g

VEGETARIAN AND VEGAN RECIPES

Potato Gratin

Servings: 4 / Cooking Time: 20 Mins.

Ingredients:

- 2 large potatoes, sliced thinly
- 5½ tbsp. cream
- 2 eggs
- 1 tbsp. plain flour
- ½ C. cheddar cheese, grated

Directions:

1. Press "Power Button" of Ninja Foodi Digital Air Fry Oven and turn the dial to select "Air Fry" mode.
2. Press "Time Button" and again turn the dial to set the cooking time to 10 minutes.
3. Now push "Temp Button" and rotate the dial to set the temperature at 355 degrees F.
4. Press "Start/Pause" button to start.
5. When the unit beeps to show that it is preheated, open the lid.
6. Arrange the potato slices in the air fry basket and insert in the oven.
7. Meanwhile, in a bowl, add cream, eggs and flour and mix until a thick sauce forms.
8. When cooking time is complete, open the lid and remove the potato slices from the basket.
9. Divide the potato slices in 4 ramekins evenly and top with the egg mixture evenly, followed by the cheese.
10. Press "Power Button" of Ninja Foodi Digital Air Fry Oven and turn the dial to select "Air Fry" mode.
11. Press "Time Button" and again turn the dial to set the cooking time to 10 minutes.
12. Now push "Temp Button" and rotate the dial to set the temperature at 390 degrees F.
13. Arrange the ramekins in the air fry basket and insert in the oven.
14. Press "Start/Pause" button to start.
15. When cooking time is complete, open the lid and remove the ramekins from the oven.
16. Serve warm.
17. Serving Suggestions: Serve this gratin with fresh lettuce.
18. Variation Tip: Make sure to cut the potato slices thinly.

Nutrition: *Calories: 233 Fat: 8g Sat Fat: 4.3g Carbohydrates: 31.3g Fiber: 4.5g Sugar: 2.7g Protein: 9.7g*

Baked Potatoes

Servings: 2 / Cooking Time: 1 Hour

Ingredients:

- 1 tbsp. peanut oil
- 2 large potatoes, scrubbed
- ½ tsp. of coarse sea salt

Directions:

1. Preheat your air fryer to 200 degrees C or 400 degrees F.
2. Brush peanut oil on your potatoes.
3. Sprinkle some salt.
4. Keep them in the basket of your air fryer.
5. Cook the potatoes for an hour.

Nutrition: *Calories 360, Carbohydrates 64g, Cholesterol 0mg, Total Fat 8g, Protein 8g, Sugar 3g, Fiber 8g, Sodium 462mg*

Vegetarian And Vegan Recipes

Potato-skin Wedges

Servings: 4 / Cooking Time: 30 Mins.

Ingredients:

- 4 medium potatoes
- 3 tbsp. of canola oil
- 1 C. of water
- ¼ tsp. black pepper, ground
- 1 tsp. paprika

Directions:

1. Keep the potatoes in a big-sized pot. Add salted water and keep covered. Boil.
2. Bring down the heat to medium. Let it simmer. It should become tender.
3. Drain the water on.
4. Keep in a bowl and place in the refrigerator until it becomes cool.
5. Bring together the paprika, oil, salt, and black pepper in a bowl.
6. Now cut the potatoes into small quarters. Toss them into your mixture.
7. Preheat your air fryer to 200 degrees C or 400 degrees F.
8. Add half of the wedges of potato into the fryer basket. Keep them skin-down. Don't overcrowd.
9. Cook for 15 minutes. It should become golden brown.

Nutrition: *Calories 276, Carbohydrates 38g, Cholesterol 0mg, Total Fat 12g, Protein 4g, Sugar 2g, Fiber 5g, Sodium 160mg*

Glazed Mushrooms

Servings: 4 / Cooking Time: 15 Mins.

Ingredients:

- ¼ C. soy sauce
- ¼ C. honey
- ¼ C. balsamic vinegar
- 2 garlic cloves, chopped finely
- ½ tsp. red pepper flakes, crushed
- 18 oz. fresh Cremini mushrooms, halved

Directions:

1. In a bowl, place the soy sauce, honey, vinegar, garlic and red pepper flakes and mix well. Set aside.
2. Place the mushroom into the greased baking pan in a single layer.
3. Press "Power Button" of Ninja Foodi Digital Air Fry Oven and turn the dial to select "Air Bake" mode.
4. Press "Time Button" and again turn the dial to set the cooking time to 15 minutes.
5. Now push "Temp Button" and rotate the dial to set the temperature at 350 degrees F.
6. Press "Start/Pause" button to start.
7. When the unit beeps to show that it is preheated, open the lid.
8. Insert the baking pan in oven.
9. After 8 minutes of cooking, place the honey mixture in baking pan and toss to coat well.
10. When cooking time is complete, open the lid and transfer the mushrooms onto serving plates.
11. Serve hot.
12. Serving Suggestions: Topping of fresh chives or marjoram gives a delish touch to mushrooms.
13. Variation Tip: Maple syrup will be an excellent substitute for honey.

Nutrition: Calories: 113 Fat: 0.2g Sat Fat: 0g Carbohydrates: 24.7g Fiber: 1g Sugar: 20g Protein: 4.4g

Sweet & Tangy Mushrooms

Servings: 4 / Cooking Time: 15 Mins.

Ingredients:

- ¼ C. soy sauce
- ¼ C. honey
- ¼ C. balsamic vinegar
- 2 garlic cloves, chopped finely
- ½ tsp. red pepper flakes, crushed
- 18 oz. cremini mushrooms, halved

Directions:

1. In a bowl, place the soy sauce, honey, vinegar, garlic and red pepper flakes and mix well. Set aside.
2. Place the mushroom into the greased baking pan in a single layer.
3. Press "Power Button" of Ninja Foodi Digital Air Fry Oven and turn the dial to select the "Air Bake" mode.
4. Press the Time button and again turn the dial to set the cooking time to 15 minutes.
5. Now push the Temp button and rotate the dial to set the temperature at 350 degrees F.
6. Press "Start/Pause" button to start.
7. When the unit beeps to show that it is preheated, open the lid.
8. Insert the baking pan in oven.
9. After 8 minutes of cooking, place the honey mixture in baking pan and toss to coat well.
10. Serve hot.

Nutrition: *Calories 113 Total Fat 0.2 g Saturated Fat 0 g Cholesterol 0 mg Sodium 9.8 mg Total Carbs 24.7 g Fiber 1 g Sugar 20 g Protein 4.4 g*

Roasted Vegetables

Servings: 4 / Cooking Time: 20 Mins.

Ingredients:

- 1 yellow squash, cut into small pieces
- 1 red bell pepper, seeded and cut into small pieces
- ¼ oz. mushrooms, cleaned and halved
- 1 tbsp. of extra-virgin olive oil
- 1 zucchini, cut into small pieces

Directions:

1. Preheat your air fryer. Keep the squash, red bell pepper, and mushrooms in a bowl.
2. Add the black pepper, salt, and olive oil. Combine well by tossing.
3. Keep the vegetables in your fryer basket.
4. Air fry them for 15 minutes. They should get roasted. Stir about halfway into the roasting time.

Nutrition: *Calories 89, Carbohydrates 8g, Cholesterol 0mg, Total Fat 5g, Protein 3g, Sugar 4g, Fiber 2.3g, Sodium 48mg*

Spicy Butternut Squash

Servings: 4 / Cooking Time: 20 Mins.

Ingredients:

- 1 medium butternut squash, peeled, seeded and cut into chunk
- 2 tsp. cumin seeds
- 1/8 tsp. garlic powder
- 1/8 tsp. chili flakes, crushed
- Salt and freshly ground black pepper, to taste
- 1 tbsp. olive oil
- 2 tbsp. pine nuts
- 2 tbsp. fresh cilantro, chopped

Directions:

1. In a bowl, mix together the squash, spices, and oil.
2. Press "Power Button" of Ninja Foodi Digital Air Fry Oven and turn the dial to select "Air Fry" mode.
3. Press "Time Button" and again turn the dial to set the cooking time to 20 minutes.
4. Now push "Temp Button" and rotate the dial to set the temperature at 375 degrees F.
5. Press "Start/Pause" button to start.
6. When the unit beeps to show that it is preheated, open the lid and grease the air fry basket.
7. Arrange the squash chunks into the prepared air fry basket and insert in the oven.
8. When cooking time is complete, open the lid and transfer the squash chunks onto serving plates.
9. Serve hot with the garnishing of pine nuts and cilantro.
10. Serving Suggestions: Serve with a sprinkle of sweet dried cranberries.
11. Variation Tip: you can microwave the butternut squash for 2-3 mins to make it softer and easier to remove the skin.

Nutrition: Calories: 191 Fat: 7g Sat Fat: 0.8g Carbohydrates: 34.3g Fiber: 6g Sugar: 6.4g Protein: 3.7g

Fried Chickpeas

Servings: 4 / Cooking Time: 20 Mins.

Ingredients:

- 1 can chickpeas, rinsed and drained
- 1 tbsp. olive oil
- 1 tbsp. of nutritional yeast
- 1 tsp. garlic, granulated
- 1 tsp. of smoked paprika

Directions:

1. Spread the chickpeas on paper towels. Cover using a second paper towel later.
2. Allow them to dry for half an hour.
3. Preheat your air fryer to 180 degrees C or 355 degrees F.
4. Bring together the nutritional yeast, chickpeas, smoked paprika, olive oil, salt, and garlic in a mid-sized bowl. Coat well by tossing.
5. Now add your chickpeas to the fryer.
6. Cook for 16 minutes until they turn crispy. Shake them in 4-minute intervals.

Nutrition: *Calories 133, Carbohydrates 17g, Cholesterol 0mg, Total Fat 5g, Protein 5g, Sugar 0g, Fiber 4g, Sodium 501mg*

Printed in Great Britain
by Amazon

12272764R00038